TOM CLARK

JUNKETS ON A SAD PLANET

SCENES FROM THE LIFE OF
JOHN KEATS

BLACK SPARROW PRESS   SANTA ROSA   1994

ACKNOWLEDGEMENTS

Some of these pieces first appeared in *The American Poetry Review,*
Arshile, Exquisite Corpse, Five Fingers Review, Gas, Long News: In
the Short Century, and *Rain City Review.*

Cover image: John Keats, from the life mask by Benjamin Robert
Haydon, 1816 (photograph by Christopher Oxford).

Black Sparrow Press books are printed on acid-free paper.

LIBRARY OF CONGRESS CATALOGING-IN-PUBLICATION DATA
Clark, Tom, 1941–
    Junkets on a sad planet : scenes from the life of John Keats / Tom Clark.
       p.   cm.
    ISBN 0-87685-918-X (cloth trade ed.) : $25.00. — ISBN 0-87685-917-1 (paper ed.)
: $13.00 — ISBN 0-87685-919-8 (signed cloth ed.) : $30.00
    1. Keats, John, 1795-1821—Poetry. 2. Poets, English—19th century—Poetry.
I. Title.
PS3553.L29J86   1993
821'.7—dc20   93-43557
                                                                CIP

A Poet is the most unpoetical of any thing in existence;
because he has no Identity—he is continually in . . . and
filling some other Body . . .

—Keats to Richard Woodhouse, October 27, 1818

Mimesis, understood as the non-conceptual affinity of a
subjective creation with its objective unposited other . . .
What the artist contributes to expression is his ability
to mimic, which sets free in him the expressed substance.

—Theodor Adorno, *Aesthetic Theory*

The poet John Keats is a master of mimetic figuration, whose
mature art provides insistent, intense expressive habitation of
the living world, and whose conjectural proposals of the figurative
aspects of a poet's life, its quality as fable—foregrounding the
problem of suffering as a thematic both within and without the
work—offer us a unique readout of the experience and mean-
ing of being a modern poet.

Junkets on a Sad Planet—the title appropriates his friend Leigh
Hunt's nickname for Keats, a play on his Cockney pronunciation
of his own name—is an extended reflection on the fable of the
modern poet's life, as Keats lived it. The book may be read by
turns as a poetic novel, biography in verse, allegorical masque,
historical oratorio for several voices.

Basic facts of Keats' life story—dates and characters—are
taken for granted in some of the pieces. For readers unfamiliar
with those facts, a capsule chronology and thumbnail cast list
have been placed at the front of the book.

Table of Contents

CODA: ECHO AND VARIATION

JUNKETS ON A SAD PLANET:
SCENES FROM THE LIFE OF JOHN KEATS

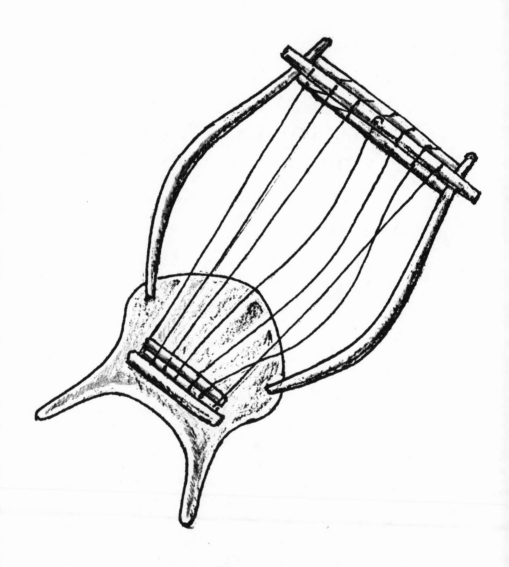

Historical Events

October 31, 1795. John Keats, son of Thomas Keats, a stableman and ostler, and Frances Jennings, is born on the premises of the Swan and Hoop inn and livery stables, Moorfields Pavement, London. His brothers George and Tom are born in 1797 and 1799, his sister Fanny in 1803.

1802. Keats is enrolled at Clarke's School, Enfield.

April 16, 1804. Thomas Keats, John's father, dies after a fall from his horse. Two months later, Frances Jennings Keats remarries, to William Rawlings, a clerk. Her parents, John and Alice Jennings, take custody of the Keats children at their home in Enfield, north of London; after John Jennings' death the following year, the children move with Alice Jennings to a neighboring village, Edmonton.

March 10, 1810. Frances Jennings Keats, John's mother, dies of tuberculosis.

1811. Keats signs on as an apprentice to a surgeon, Joseph Hammond of Edmonton.

1814. Upon the death of Alice Jennings, Richard Abbey, proprietor of a London counting-house and tea brokerage firm, becomes legal guardian of John Keats and his siblings. Keats writes his first poems.

1815. Keats matriculates as a medical student at Guy's Hospital, London, and is appointed a surgical dresser.

1816. Keats passes qualifying exams as an apothecary and receives a license to practice, but by the end of the year gives up medicine for poetry. His first published poem appears in Leigh Hunt's *Examiner*. He takes up residence briefly at Dean Street in the Borough and then, by the middle of

November, with his brothers, at 76 Cheapside. Between October and December he writes "On First Looking into Chapman's Homer," and meets Joseph Severn, Leigh Hunt, Benjamin Robert Haydon, and John Hamilton Reynolds. Hunt bestows upon him the familiar nickname "Junkets," a play on Keats' Cockney pronunciation of his own name.

1817. Keats publishes his first book, *Poems*, and in March moves with his brothers to Well Walk, Hampstead. Between April and November, reading Shakespeare intensely, writing steadily, and moving restlessly from place to place (The Isle of Wight, Margate, Canterbury, Hastings, back to Hampstead, Oxford, Hampstead again, Surrey), he drafts *Endymion*. Meets, by the end of the year, Benjamin Bailey, Charles Wentworth Dilke, Charles Brown, and Wordsworth.

1818. Keats hears William Hazlitt lecture on the English poets at the Surrey Institution. In early March, he hastens to Devon to join his ailing brother Tom at the resort town of Teignmouth, and stays into April. *Endymion*, revised earlier this year, is published by Taylor and Hessey, and negatively reviewed, most notably by *Blackwood's* (May) and the *Quarterly* (October). In June, Keats sees off his newly-married brother George, and wife Georgiana, on their departure from Liverpool to settle in America. He takes off thence with Charles Brown on a walking tour of the Lake Country, Scotland and the north of Ireland. In early August, a chronic sore throat causes him to return alone from Inverness. Back in Hampstead, he finds his brother Tom seriously ill. He starts "Hyperion" and nurses Tom at 1 Well Walk until the latter's death on December 1. Thereafter he moves across Hampstead to Wentworth Place, where he becomes a paying houseguest of Brown. He spends Christmas day with the family of a new friend and Hampstead neighbor, Fanny Brawne.

1819. Keats writes "The Eve of St. Agnes" on a January visit to Chichester. In April and May he writes "La Belle Dame sans Merci" and the Nightingale, Melancholy, and Grecian Urn odes. He spends most of August and September with Brown in Winchester, where he works on "The Fall of Hyperion" and "Lamia," and writes the Ode to Autumn. In fall or early winter, back in Hampstead, he becomes secretly engaged to marry Fanny Brawne.

1820. In February, coming home to Wentworth Place after a coach trip into the city, he suffers a severe hemorrhage, first ominous signal of encroaching tuberculosis. When Brown rents Wentworth Place for the summer, Keats takes rooms at 2 Wesleyan Place, Kentish Town. After another severe hemorrhage in June, he is moved to Leigh Hunt's house at nearby Mortimer Terrace. In July, his book *Lamia, Isabella, The Eve of St. Agnes and Other Poems* is published by Taylor and Hessey, and receives positive reviews. In August he is taken in by the Brawnes, now occupying the house adjoining Brown's at Wentworth Place, and spends his last month in England with them. Ordered by his doctors to seek the warmer climate of Italy for the winter, he sails on September 18 from Gravesend on the *Maria Crowther*, accompanied by the artist Joseph Severn. After a difficult voyage they reach Naples on October 21, and spend ten days quarantined on shipboard in the harbor there due to a typhoid epidemic in London. Traveling on by coach to Rome, they arrive on November 15 and occupy an apartment overlooking the Piazza di Spagna. Keats is mortally ill.

February 23, 1821. Keats dies in Rome at eleven in the evening. Three days later, he is buried at dawn in the English Cemetery there.

Characters

Richard Abbey—London businessman appointed by the estate of Alice Jennings, John Keats' grandmother, as trustee of her estate and legal guardian of the Keats children. As to his handling of their financial affairs, generally distrusted by Keats.

Benjamin Bailey (1791–1853)—An undergraduate theological student in 1817 when he met Keats, befriended him, and hosted him at Magdalen Hall, Oxford; ordained and appointed curate in Carlisle, 1819.

Fanny Brawne (1800–1865)—Met Keats sometime in 1818, when her family rented Charles Brown's house at Wentworth Place, Hampstead; was his next-door-neighbor as of April 1819, when the Brawnes rented Charles Dilke's adjoining house on the same plot; and also his secret fiancée, perhaps as of October that same year.

Charles Armitage Brown (1787–1842)—Adventurer and entrepreneur, merchant voyager, playwright, householder, and after the death of Tom Keats in late 1818, Keats' landlord at Wentworth Place, Hampstead; met Keats in 1817 and toured the North with him in the summer of the following year.

Charles Cowden Clarke (1787–1877)—Son of John Clarke, headmaster of Clarke's School at Enfield; as a teacher at the school and later as a friend, an instrumental figure in Keats' early development, introducing him to both the great poets of the past and important living literary practitioners like Leigh Hunt.

Charles Wentworth Dilke (1789–1864)—Civil servant and private scholar; with wife Maria, in the years 1817–1819 frequently entertained Keats at their house on a plot adjoining that of his old schoolmate, Charles Brown, at Wentworth Place, Hampstead.

William Haslam (1795–1851)—Enfield schoolmate and family friend of the Keats boys, later a London grocer; it was Haslam who, unable to go himself, recruited Joseph Severn to accompany Keats to Italy in 1821, and helped set up their voyage.

Benjamin Robert Haydon (1786–1846)—Epic painter who championed the English acquisition of the Elgin Marbles and captured Keats' head in his monumental *Christ's Entry into Jerusalem.*

Leigh Hunt (1784–1859)—Radical editor (*The Examiner*), indefatigable journalist and journeyman poet, veteran of two years' well-publicized political imprisonment, early hero of Keats as an emblem of liberty ("Libertas"); then, as of October 1816, his literary patron; and later a host to him in his final days in England.

Fanny Keats (1803–1889)—John Keats' sister, kept in generally unhappy circumstances by the Keats children's legal guardian, Abbey, until her coming of age in 1824.

George Keats (1797–1841)—After attending Clarke's School and working briefly for Abbey as a clerk, lived with Tom and John in London and at 1 Well Walk, Hampstead, until his 1818 marriage to Georgiana Wylie and subsequent departure for America; landing in Kentucky, he lost his capital on a commercial enterprise sponsored by John James Audubon, and briefly returned to London in 1820 to raise funds out of his (and John's) share of Tom's estate.

Tom Keats (1799–1818)—After leaving school, worked briefly with George at Abbey's financial establishment in the city; upon falling ill in 1818, was nursed in Devon early that year, first by George, then John, and again by John in the fall at Well Walk, Hampstead, where he died on December 1.

Vincent Novello (1781–1861)—London musician and social host, friend of Leigh Hunt.

John Hamilton Reynolds (1794–1852)—Insurance man, prominent reviewer, fashionable poet, ultimately an unsuccessful lawyer, befriended Keats in 1817 and introduced him to Bailey, Brown, Dilke and Rice, among others.

James Rice (1792–c. 1833)—Lawyer and amateur literary man, prominent figure in a convivial card-playing club attended by Keats as of October 1817.

Joseph Severn (1793–1879)—Journeyman painter who, though previously only a casual friend (since 1816) to Keats, volunteered to accompany him to Italy in September 1820, and nursed him tirelessly thenceforward to his death.

Horace Smith (1779–1849)—Stockbroker, sometime writer, member of Leigh Hunt's circle.

John Taylor (1781–1864)—Editorial half of the publishing partnership of Taylor and Hessey, Keats' publishers and patrons.

Richard Woodhouse (1788–1834)—Lawyer, scholar; friend, voluntary literary secretary and generous patron of Keats as of c. 1817.

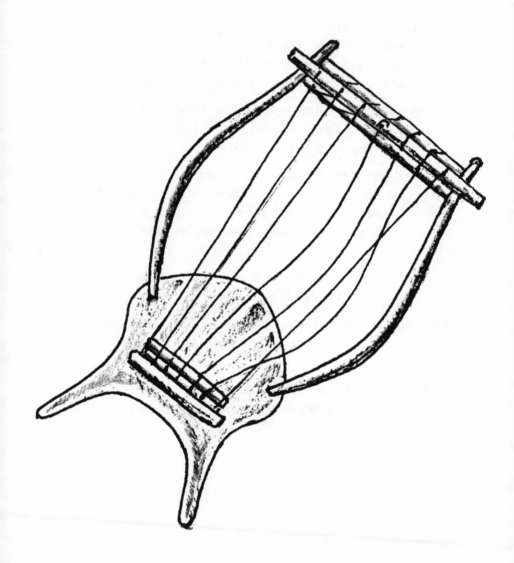

But even now I am perhaps not speaking from myself,
but from some character in whose soul I now live.

—Keats to Richard Woodhouse, October 27, 1818

One of the most mysterious of semi-speculations is, one
would suppose, that of one mind imagining into another.

—Keats' undated marginalia to *Paradise Lost*

Prelude: The Power of Song

Hermes found an empty tortoise shell on the beach, strung seven strings through the holes. Light shimmered on the strings like flying fish, and they made sweet modal sounds when plucked by nothing more than a passing breeze.

Hermes swapped this instrument to Apollo for a magic healing staff entwined with snakes. The staff also possessed an ability to render its owner airborne, but Apollo did not feel cheated in the exchange, for now he possessed the power of song, and his tongue tasted sweet as honey in his mouth.

Light years passed. Space became time. Apollo passed on the power of song to his son, Orpheus, alerting him as he did so to the special concealed defect of this gift: You could die for the power of song, yet not kill with it.

1. Possession

Pegasus Jockey

Born over a stable, a stableboy's son,
A boxer in my youth, tiny as Tom Thumb,
With a naval officer in the family,
Apprenticed as an apothecary,
Later on it is proposed to me that
I become a commercial man in the hat
Or tea trades, or write popular plays,
Or become a doctor on the high seas,
Plying plasters on an Indiaman,
But I spare myself confinement in all
Those yawning quarters by throwing
Myself completely into the nervous
Excitement of riding the little horse
Poetry, with its shoes kicking in the stars.

Yonder's Wall (1804)

The family name means herdsman. My father was an ostler. And I was born above a stable, in my parents' bedroom at the Swan and Hoop. My mother's father's previous prosperity in the inn and livery trade, passed on and in my father's time not yet lost to us, gave my early childhood, our stable days, a stability, if I may pun on my life. Under stars of minor magnitude I was born, a stableman's son, and taught myself to ride the little horse— not Pegasus the winged stallion but Equuleus the colt, whose bucking hoof, the bronco star Kitalpha, flashes past Poetry's turned up nose. And my star fell from its ascension early in those same mean streets around the Swan and Hoop where I scrapped and tumbled, and through which, in my eighth year, my father's horse came home one night, he having fallen from it somewhere near London Wall.

Cockney Childhood

At play among the minor magnitudes as a child
Above the Swan and Hoop Keats toys with stars,
Sky bodies dance like tops and jacks in agile
Imaginings of his small street boxer's hands.

Rising over London Wall, anchoring the Summer Triangle,
Vega, a bluish white star of major magnitude in Lyra,
Is conspicuous in its passage from the south
Over the smoky fogbound eighteenth century town.

Romance

From my Infancy I had no mother. After my father died, and she left Rawlings, she had no money, she lived with another man, a Jew at Enfield, named Abraham, it was known to common persons of the town—a shame to me, and disturbing when in my growing defensive melancholy I got in scrapes to keep those things unspoken of and her name a matter of some honor, for it still was to me—and when going to the market through the mud of the streets she'd had a way of hiking her skirts up higher than she needed to, it was a growing pain that in our separation inspired me to the energetic combat of the schoolyard. She was in distress, and I would fight for her, and protect her, possessively, like a knight out of Spenser, yet disinterested, as in Romance, with my naked sword.

Quietness

My mother fell into a consumption. I cooked her meals for her, sat in a chair and read her novels, administered the drug called Quietness that seemed to lift her not only from her pain but from herself, for a few minutes, or an hour, and with a cool cloth wiped away the tangled strands of grimy hair that fell across her fevered brow—that face doubly dear to me—because for those several years, after my father's fatal fall, and the horrid interloper Rawlings, a wretched clerk whose true trade it was to prey on widows, then later the other disgraces, the tales of her being kept by the Jew at Enfield, and my grandmother telling us nothing of her, we had supposed her forever gone—and then her coming back a sad wanderer, drinking brandy—this dying beauty coiling in her pain upon the drenched bedsheets—I believe it was her seeming not so much my mother as some marvelous revenant out of a ghost story or a tragedy, forced to undergo its end a second time, that made my fear so grave, my love for her so strong, and my grief in the later days back at school so unnerving—so that during study hours I hid behind the master's desk to dwell unto myself, in my anguish over losing her, while the other boys and the master himself kindly waited upon me, and the room fell hushed.

Possession

> "I have two luxuries to brood over in my walks,
> your Loveliness and the hour of my death."
>
> —Keats to Fanny Brawne, July 25, 1819

She was bedridden, tanked on brandy and
Opium, in pain, disheveled, beautiful,
And for the first time unarguably physically *there*
As he sat up long nights in the armchair,
A strange adolescent beside her strange body,
The only one of which he ever wished to take possession,
So that later when he huddled speechless in his grief
Behind the master's desk, and the whole class
Fell into a hush out of sympathy with his loss,
He knew they had no idea how unfortunate a one
He was, or what he would give to have her back—
His life, and the sexual form in which it possessed him.

Sidereal Study   (The Dormitory, Clarke's School, Enfield, 1809 or 1810)

Turning, as a boy, to books, and to woods and fields,
Courting the genius of language and the *genius loci,*
Directing into the cosmos of his own driven summoning
All that feeling displaced from its lost human objects,

Losing himself into the moment of his studenthood,
Prosing the *Aeneid,* learning Lemprière by heart,
Scanning, while downstairs Cowden Clarke practiced Mozart,
The night sky, schematic anatomy of a mythic

Pre-world with its promise of high morning heroism and its
        even
Higher paradigms of expanding darkness—
Already by some poet instinct knowing that here in the
        universe
The evening is young, there are still not enough stars.

Experience (Inside)

With this living hand this moment I was writing, and with the other holding to my mouth a nectarine—good god how fine—it went down soft pulpy, slushy, oozy—all its delicious embonpoint melted down my throat like a large beatified strawberry.

What I like best to feel is the inside of a billiard ball, or the luscious spheroid of a plum.

What I like best to look at, when I am out walking, are the waves the wind makes in the wheat when it moves across the fields above the ground.

Chapman's Homer (Cortez, Jr.)   (October 1816)

The handsome calfbound folio Chapman's Homer
Lent to Clarke by the generous classicist from the *Times*
Ended up in Little Keats the doctor-poet's
Hot excited hands, in their first symposium
At Clerkenwell. He pitched himself upon the floor
Before it, and with growing emotion followed
The voyage of Odysseus out upon the poetry,
The shipwrecked hero runnynosed and gasping
On the Elizabethan esperanto shore

Making him cry out with identifying feeling,
Bowled over by great genius' overflow
Which soon had soaked his soul through
And caught his heart up in its salty cordage—
And rolling home at dawn with dauntless
Seaman's gait, sensed he'd travelled gold
Realms, and seen amazing states and kingdoms,
Though he was not yet twenty-one years old,
And only about to embark on that exhausting trip.

2. Debut

Brother of the Quill (Grub Street News)   (1816)

Grub Street, home to curious hackney authors
Baptized me in the language of its canting crew—
Rufflers, Hookers, Fraters, Jarkmen, Patricoes,
Upright Men, Anglers, Rogues, Wild Rogues,

Fresh Water Mariners, Whip Jackets, Drummerers,
Drunken Tinkers, Abrams, and their Walking Morts,
Autem Morts, Bawdy Baskets, Glimmerers for Fire,
Doxies, Delles, Kinching Morts and Kinching Coes.

Among those mean streets beneath the bells of Bow
I learnt to patter flash, to cut a sham and fling
And mill and flam and hum and job the average cove;
To counterfeit a gravity and understanding

I did not have, I mastered next the Dog Latin and
Gallipot vocabulary of the apothecary trade;
So that later, when I moved on in the world and found
The whole crooked history was being authored

By a malicious hand, my quill-brother's background
Among the canting crew tempered my surprise—
Knowing your best of truth in this world's always
Lying intelligence, or Grub Street News.

Morbidity   (Guy's Hospital, Fall 1816)

I believe surgery is getting to be too
much for me—after another prolonged horror
session, watching the momentarily living
dispatched into a bloody underworld
of tangled viscera, in which I grasp,
like fishing noodles from some ghastly soup,
for vessels severed by the butcher Lucas,

I dream the resurrection men who angle
like so many shady Izaak Waltons
for dead souls floating in the River
to be sold to Guy's, where I dissect them,
are my doubles, doppelgängers in
the eternity library, readers of
my surgical nightmare Book of the Dead.

Dark Commerce

I feel the world—even before I commence
on the literary scene—somehow
a lie—deceitful—sordid—
already at Guy's, a sense of fetor,
dark commerce, and a business in
men's hearts of the grotesque—
a trading in life and death—
as the resurrection men—so many
shady Izaak Waltons, staying
like Troilus for waftage
on the Stygian banks—stray-trolling
for marketable cadavers
among the casual graves and night
soils of the Thames shore—

Imagination   **(Leaving Guy's Hospital,
November 1816)**

It was imagination, after one
particularly trying temporal
artery ligation in which he felt
outside himself looking down at the operating
table from a strange vantage
point up in the far corner of
the theatre, beyond death, that
made him lay down the surgeon's
lancet. And when, soon after,
he took Leigh Hunt's cold-fishy
soft palm into his own warm
agitated hand, he could still sense
the grave after-touch of mortal
knowledge, the dead clay and soiled
night tissues of the cadaver
mongers, the resurrection men,
in culture's welcoming grasp.

Head in Clouds

After slapping on him the presumptuously
Familiar diminutive moniker "Junkets,"
The wasted child prodigy gone silly bohemian, Hunt,
Engaged his new protégé in a poetry match, shouting Bravo!

As Keats read out his *The poetry of earth is never*
Dead, catching the phase change from drowsy summer to
    sudden
First frosts of autumn, and gauging our stars' great distance,
And the hanging fire of a cruising Cockney moon

Beamed in his flattered eye as he breezed home with that
Rolling sailor's attitude that made him appear dauntless
Despite his size, cocky, drunk with delight,
The six or more miles from Hampstead to Cheapside.

Debut   (Vale of Health, Hampstead, Fall 1816)

That October of his coming of age, he abandoned medicine
And the idea of doing something great for humankind.
Taken up by Leigh Hunt and the dilettanti, he embarked
In a frail craft powered by his intense language drive,

Purposefully, his heart soaked through with poetry,
Like Odysseus across the restless waves of Chapman's
     Homer
On his new era existence voyage toward genius, with
The hopeful innocence of a lamb led on fate tides.

Accompanied in his awed silence by Clarke, that first cool,
Clear autumn early evening, to the Vale of Health,
Where Hunt's busy little white cottage culture industry
     flourished,
With accelerated step, all small talk lapsing,

The long legged cricketer Clarke struggling to keep up,
Keats stayed speechless as they walked along,
His mute gaze alert as a forest creature's
A hungry eaglet fixity in his eyes,

Light auburn curls flaring up like softest plumage
In the gently stirring twilight breeze,
Rapt, anxious, lost in anticipation,
Hushed as if approaching some ancient sacrifice.

At Hunt's Mozart was played on a tinkling pianoforte,
And poetry repeatedly flowed from the lips of men
Who babbled with the noisy children, who were strange,
Whose names the visitor knew from literary magazines.

Keeping himself apart, modestly infatuated, Keats sat
Crosslegged in a chair, stroked his instep, was curious,
Now and then put in some quiet remark,
Indulged Hunt's presumption in calling him Junkets,

Soon won everyone over—as the hours "Ere the morn
Of Truth" wore on, fitting into the scene like a delightful
Pocket charm, a miniature gem surrounded
In its setting by the prior luminaries of those hours,

The sympathetic lightweight liberal Hunt, a wasted prodigy
Still fey and silly as a faery in a masque
Despite his debts, his neurasthenia, his prison sentence;
The quicksilver poetaster Reynolds, a Mercury

With clay heels; Haydon, the blunt, myopic Minotaur
With a perpetual hankering for going down in history;
And the facile aethereal thoroughbred Shelley, shying
Like a Pegasus from the world on paper liberty wings.

Later, coming home to Dean Street, Keats walked on air
Setting sail at a footpad's pace, with the cricketer
Clarke struggling to keep up, across the Heath, drunk
With delight, under Lyra's frosty autumn stars.

Hero Worship (The Better Side of the Common in Keats)

(Fall 1816)

Had Keats not been picked up by the dilettanti (Hunt,
    Haydon)
Would he have had the nerve to absurdly foreshorten his
    own life
And fortune by throwing over his medical career for
    poetry?
His legal guardian, Abbey, told him he was being silly, but
    he was simply acting out
His infatuation with the pseudo-radical bohemianism of
    Hunt.
Infected briefly with Haydon's inflationary vision
He tiptoed selfconsciously on the brink of high importance
To write "Great spirits now on earth are sojourning."
But when Haydon pumped further hot
Air into the personality balloon by promising
To send the sonnet to young Junkets' hero
Wordsworth, the better side of the common in
Keats came out and he demurred, "You put me out of
    breath!"

Ambition (1817)

Having chosen poetry, it was necessary for him next to make a fool out of himself, which he proceeded then to do. He and Hunt crowned one another with laurel and wrote lame sonnets: afterwards Keats' own attempt would make him wince. Still when Haydon the blind minotaur thereupon convinced him the grand heroic mode was the only way to go, he swelled with ambition, took up Shelley's competitive challenge and resolved to crank out a four-thousand-line poem, though he didn't yet have the thought to fill one sonnet. These were the days of attendance at Horace Smith's and Novello's, when being articled to the culture industry made poetry appear to Keats merely a new form of apprenticeship to a commercial trade, something no one else in it dared recognize (Haydon, contemptuous of mere business, had him cut out the reference to "marts" in "Great spirits now on earth . . ."). Thus began *Endymion.*

Sensitive

Wordsworth at forty-seven was snappish,
vain and grumpy. Keats at twenty-two
was anxious, brilliant, empathic, moody,
confused, and too sensitive for his own good.
At their meeting presided over by Haydon,
Wordsworth told Keats his Hymn to Pan
was no more than a pretty piece of paganism
and as Haydon shrewdly noted, Keats
actually trembled, like the string of
a lyre when it has been touched.

Endymion

Endymion: it is all one moon who in
The innumerable phases of women

Turns to kiss him. And when, guilty over
His serial betrayals, he feels muddled,

It is the mawkish young author who rushes
In to assist him. We hold our breath for him.

His dreams fill up with melting women who
Will have their way with him, in the dark

They are all alike. He may not wake up soon,
No one may ever wake up again.

For fear all women will stop sleeping
With him, nature presses a finger to her lips.

The Moon Goddess

In the myth of fate, a manly hunter looked at a naked
Moonwoman, and was torn to pieces. So much for great
Mythic sex. A tale of protracted adolescence, *Endymion*
Told the story of a mortal who was allowed sex

With a goddess, and never paid the price for it,
A violation of the myth of fate. Keats
Later chalked it up to inexperience,
In a preface intended to head the reviewers off

At the pass. But the myth continued to spin
Its story, like poisoned cotton floss.
His Cockney apothecary-poet background, leaked
To Lockhart of *Blackwood's* by the bumbling

Oxford parson Bailey, became the sheet anchor
By which *Endymion* was sunk, and his
Divine Woman refused to have sex with him,
Even at the bottom of the ocean.

Incident at Hastings (1817)

Her smuggling history, and the diverting sea
Air that shored up the old fort town of Hastings
Nerved him with the courage of an infantryman
As he warmed with Mrs. Jones at the New England Bank.

Though he said a woman likes to be forced to
Do a thing by a fine fellow, Keats wouldn't.
How could she have warmed with him at Hastings
Had not Mrs. Jones harbored an intent so to warm?

Evergreens   (November 1817)

To finish his romance that fall he packed up again,
Went off to Box Hill, got a room over stables
Above the shining Mole, under chalk downs,
In heavy cover of elm and box and yew,
And when the first night the cool star light
Rushed in like some memory of the Swan
And Hoop, burst from his room, raced up the steep
Hill through the yew heavy with the coming
Down of the moon, the red berries lighting
Up the dark under that thin diamond
Peaked moon, no bigger than an unobserved
Star parked in the night's hangar, for
A glimpse into the penetralium.

The Mummer's Play
(Negative Capability)

(December 1817)

Tom was losing weight and spitting blood now, the skin over his small delicate facial bones taking on a waxen transparency that could not but give rise to a premonitory shudder in his brothers, who of course had seen all this once before (though George, two years younger, professed not to recall). Tom was taken off by George to Devon, for the improvement of his breathing. Two weeks went by. Keats sat in the cheap seats at the Drury Lane Christmas pantomime in his customary attitude of wild surmise as the hay-filled sleeve batted into the clown playing the leaf and the flower, and the common crowd roared. Afterwards he and Dilke walked on ahead of Brown. Left alone upstairs at Well Walk, the flow of his reflections broken intermittently by the howls of the wild and woolly Bentley brats downstairs, he inhaled the ambient aroma of candle fumes and worsted stockings, and as the moments passed feeling himself almost physically in their presence, watched the nib under his living hand bleed his thoughts out in a letter to his brothers.

His purpose in writing was simply to be entertaining and diverting. Shakespeare worked for that, but to get in suffering as well, though Keats still was not comfortable with the idea of confronting suffering. Like the goblin who stays not only tolerant but enamored of the natural ambiguity of things even on the eve of being driven from the hearth, he *half knew* but was in no rush to arrive at certainty. His intense pleasure in not knowing was based on the probably foolish sense that things might somehow remain free.

3. Premonitory

Tom Makes Noises About a Return to Town   (March 1818)

So I fly off to forestall him, rushing from the last of Hazlitt's talks on the English poets to the Swan With Two Necks, Lad Lane, to catch the Exeter coach. I weigh the dangers boded by a restless southeast wind against the extra two pennies a mile for an inside seat, then take an outside seat as usual. A horrendous storm blows up, swamps the coach, threatens Mr. Macadam's handiwork with a sea of mud. The sturdy-looking coachmen in their water-shedding many-caped coats suffer little more damage than their elegant equipages, but for those of us perched outside and unready for the weather this stop-and-go ordeal is hardly more comfortable than Bonaparte's forced march, and in my light jacket I am drenched along with my fellow exposed passengers. At an inn in Devon, a middle-sized girl of about fifteen greets us with a quartern of brandy. For the next sixteen-mile stage the thought of her warms me in my wet jacket. But I come down with a cold, find Devon a splashy, rainy, misty, muddy, slipshod country, and Tom much worse.

Leaving London on the Exeter Stage
(March 1818)

Out of that smoky faced and ruined town
Where common pain is washed out on the margins
Of open drains, in narrow wretched alleys
Fumes of night soil slowly decomposing,
Poisoned air and stagnant water stand
Commingled in unlit cellars of the damned,
While clerks with starved looks chart the flow
Of profit in thick black ledger books,
Red lined accounts blur before their tired eyes
Like blowing rain in the face of some exposed
Passenger traveling into a storm
Through a night raging with apprehensive
Prefiguration of further black weather—
On my rocking perch watching the world blown
Over and blown under, trees and houses torn
From ground and toppling down—the Exeter
Stage plows west into the hurricane

Submarine

Tom has taken on the pale misfeatured look our Mother came home to die with, recalling me to the sad scenes of her death and our earlier Misfortune.

The weeks go by, the town stays still enveloped in clouds. Where's the poet in this picture? Lying awake by night in the suffocating room on an airless alley by the waterfront in Teignmouth, listening to the rain with a sense of being drowned and rotted like a grain of wheat, my mind going out through the chill damp darkness to the deserted bandstand, the promenade crowded only by dancing drops of rain, the sailboats rocked by waves under black hoods of tarpaulin.

My amphibious heart, ever out of its element, keeps turning over, pulling of its sodden weight down again, into my blind waters, my melancholy lunes, identifying with Hamlet, a dying boy with two fathers, Tom dismal and forlorn and spitting blood, many doors under the ocean opening, but all dark, and leading to dark passages.

Off Season   (Spring 1818)

O Devonshire, you dwindle my moon in
Heaven, and drown me in my rainy lunes
My intellect degenerates apace
Tom looks pale and has a cough that causes
Blood to engorge his vocal chords
Stifling his voice like the kiss of a Medusa
His face turns blue, his eyes roll back in his head
Then in a moment he is himself again
But I am not, my blue devils coming on
To tease sleep out of my anxious mind,
Make eyelids ache into my fretted pillow,
By day I prowl the flat brown sand alone
Picking dully among the slick green rocks
At the foam troubled fringe of silver
Breakers that pound in from the dark sea with
Shocks that are a metronome of my mood,
If under that wide water now I would
Scarcely kick to come up to the top

Premonitory   (Teignmouth, Spring 1818)

Mariners don't think about the deeps too much.
The canvas of my reverie: maritime,
With promontory, cave, and little antique
Town that's emptied for a sacrifice.
A boat tacks around the cove and disappears
Into my mind's eye, where the scene plays over

And over: a small town beside an immense sea,
A white sail tacks around the promontory.
Mariners don't think too much about the deeps,
Poets were once thought premonitory.
The canvas of my reverie is
Maritime, with a promontory, a town:

The town has emptied for a sacrifice.
I close my eyes, but the same scene plays over:
Above the victim's head the priest suspends
A blade, light plays cleanly upon bronze,
The sun beats down, the confused heifer lows,
The pipe shrills, the bright libation flows,

Those of the faithful with weak nerves look away,
The blue paint splashed beneath a glowing sky
Bleeds across the harbor to the bobbing skiff
Whose white sail shows above the green head cliff,
Moves round the point, and seems to freeze in time
The unison hymn of sailors who forget

All that they know but their songs' chiming,
Chanting as we did when poetry was young,
Trying not to think too much about the deeps,

Our fear of death, and this abandoned town
Which itself has lost all memory of
The qualities of life vacated when we die.

God's Spy

(Lake Country and beyond,
Summer 1818)

Passing out of the smoky factory towns of the north
With their infernal mills crushing into dust the lyric as he
    knows it,
Dragging his mortal body of a thousand remaining days,
A burden to him like a dead weight, sodden, blistered,
Fleabitten, hungry, roughshod, sore of throat,
Reaching Windermere, experiencing naive speechless
    wonder
As befits the heroic amplitude of the scene,
Feeling nature's mass fall and spill like spray among the
    rocks,
The tone, the coloring, the slate, the stone, the moss,
The intellect of the place, a sullen driving power
Of unconscious energy with which to identify
That strength in himself fated to outlive himself,
He resolves henceforth to live within the eye
Completely, God's spy, presage and sentinel,
Vision so dispersed into things it becomes their language.

Windermere (June 1818)

"I cannot forget the joy, the rapture of my friend,
when he suddenly, and for the first time, became
sensible to the full effect of mountain scenery."
        —Charles Brown

After a day's hike in a dismal downpour,
Us wet to the skin, accosted by the old
Soldier in the drunken kitchen
Who asked if Brown's spectacles were for sale,

The mists cleared, larks blew cool notes over fresh
High air of the fells and the sky opened
On blue water, green islands, wild
Mountains stretching to white and purple clouds.

I went out in a boat, caught two trapped
Trout which were cooked for our dinner.
The waiter gossiped to us about Wordsworth's
Pathetic electioneering, but the sun

Going down shot through the clouds all the gold
Nature normally holds off from us
As time washes round these human shores,
And I had two views of the lake that won't fade:

The moving waters at their priestlike task
Of pure ablution, patient, watchful
Like a sort of north star which in shining can
Not cease to be steadfast and open-lidded

Over the wonders of the great power;
And diamonds sparkling on the oars, full night still
Far off, but already at this latitude
Polaris growing bright against the sky.

The two brothers he loved passing the love of women now
    going away,
George to America, Tom to somewhere even more crazy
    and strange,
He had to summon what strength he could, rise above
The loss of everything, mother, father, family, woman,
    fortune, fame;

And to overcome that fate, become, if not a god, then taller
    than he was.
He went on his walking tour of the North with Brown,
    brooding on his shortness,
Wrote Bailey that when among women he suffered severe
Revulsion due to his diminutive size. Yet half idiot by

Mossy waterfalls he might be a giant, much as those great
    ones
Who rebelled against Jove, taking a whole mass of
Black columns and binding them together in packs like
Blunt matches, in Fingal's Cave on Staffa.

Back   (Wentworth Place, Hampstead,
                                        August 1818)

Coming back down out of the clouds
bone tired, with a troublesome sore throat,
sunburnt and shabby, shoes worn out,
jacket all torn at the back,
knapsack full of gaping holes—he staggered
in from his tour of the North, fell into
a chair with a vast sigh, was given
a drink, and beamed, "Bless thee,
Bottom! Bless thee! Thou art translated!"

Quietness (II)   (August–September 1818)

"To make 4000 lines of one bare circumstance and fill
Them with poetry" was an ambition whose adolescent
Vanity rivaled that of the youth who fell in love
With the moon, and never grew up. But the poet himself,

Rushed into maturity by the experience of suffering,
Now did so, and found life a pathetic drama played
Out in a vast dark Theatre of Desolation,
Like Fingal's Cave on Staffa, where epic black

Columns slung by Titans littered the barren cavern floor,
Reducing the awed tourist to dwarf scale. Back
From his walking tour of the North he fell into a chair
At Dilke's, sighed, beamed and said he felt translated

Like Bottom. At that point the Dilkes hit him with the news:
Tom, left alone, was now much sicker than before.
Visions of his mother's last days flashing back,
Keats went to Well Walk, took up again the old

Selfsame night watch through slow, moony
Weeks of the dying Hampstead summer. Reading in
King Lear by his lamp one evening late, past the
Chapel bells' last tolling and his brother's slip from

Pain and panic into a fitful sleep induced by the
Drug called Quietness, he underscored, underscored
Again and dated on the yellowing Folio page
The phrase "Poor Tom." It was in those dark weeks

Blackwood's, leaked ominous science of his trade
Apprentice days by Bailey, dropped its fateful

70

Judgment on *Endymion*: "Back to the shop, Mr. John."
As if reeling from a blow in a prize fight,

Keats announced he was giving up poetry,
But then, even as he continued to nurse his fading,
Blood-spitting brother, himself rising from a red canvas,
He started *Hyperion,* and his great year was underway.

Mimesis (Empathy) (Fall 1818)

Troubled by this foolish complication of feeling,
Warmed by a Platonic empathy with the other half
Of my created fate, an identity to complete me,
Following my enigmatic encounter with
The possibly interesting courtesan Mrs. Jones—

To pass completely out of oneself, as if
One had no character at all—I throw
Away my personality like a too tight suit of clothes
On the retreating shore of my lost hopes
And strike out naked into the bracing wave—

My whole being miming Troilus repeating
Those lines, *I wander, like a lost soul upon*
The Stygian banks staying for waftage—and then
The first thing I know I am content to be myself again,
Here by my brother's bedside writing my poem of the dying
     gods

Dear George

Tom's identity presses on me so all day
I'm obliged to go out, and when I come in
His voice and feebleness are so trying
I must write to chase them from my mind

I plunge into abstract images to ease
Myself, but still live in a continual fever
It must be poisonous to life itself
To think of Fame or Poetry at such a time

Brass

Locked up in Well Walk with a sore throat,
Dosing myself with mercury, Tom's night cough
Wakes me with an evil metal taste
Like death on my tongue poisonous as brass.

The faint conceptions I have of poems to come
Bring the blood frequently into my throat
And I have a throbbing pain across my forehead,
The hidden spleen of night air playing itself out.

I hold my slant page full against the fading light,
The weak flame chokes on an ember, glows in
A final brief pulse before flaring up and then going out
In a frail unfurling of pale white smoke,

As the death boat prepares to embark on its erring
Fate-drift away from our firelit harbor.

Restless and Wary (Fall 1818)

Mercury for my sore throat, lamentable
Nights by my brother's bedside—through
His pained death mask our mother's face
Materializes, I feel I am waiting close upon
A restless ghost—

Who Is the Poet? Show Him! (Fall 1818)
(The Hoax)

Ever anguished and baffled by the Riddle of Creation,
And out of contact with the world those strange
Gray weeks and months as my brother Tom dies, nursing
His own broken illusions, cruel visions conjured by
A woman's false hand—which, in later days,
Reconstructing my fate, too late, I find out to be a man's . . .

4. Irresolution

Portrait of The Other (Fanny Brawne)

Elegant, graceful, silly, fashionable, a little strange—not quite
beautiful—perhaps it is the nose—the face too thin—the temper
inordinately high—the mind and spirits brimming—the mouth
troublesome—the arms good the hands badish the feet
tolerable—deep blue eyes—monstrous behavior flying out in all
directions—calling people such names—a pocket tiger—hair bare-
ly managed—a minx—yet perfect—the shape fine—speaks for-
ward as a man—like me, loves pranks and plays—and about my
height—

Sentiment (Fanny Brawne)   (Christmas Day, 1818)

Somehow I knew damaged Beauty would be his theme, giving him on the happiest day I had ever then spent the Tassie letter seal of a Greek lyre with half its strings dangling slack and broken—a gift I was right to think might pique his pride of song—which was not less than Apollo's—playing with words was then and ever after his chief pastime and pleasure—he gave me in return the little red leather diary book with reflections on the seasons by Mr. Hunt—I did not then know he had already come to abhor his association with Mr. Hunt—after Christmas dinner we stole away and for the first time spoke with each other as if one day we might be lovers finally—but then he went off to Chichester to join Brown, and wrote the Eve of St. Agnes—I've always thought the girl in the poem who longed for her amorous cavalier was his imagination of me, transformed to the less problematic dimension of poetry—for as I'd known all along it was in truth his poetry and not any woman to whom he would in the end surrender his heart—

Christmas Party   (After coming from Brawnes', December 1818)

Over a mug of grog bought by a man named Ross
A young sailor just back from Baffin Bay
Spoke of white bears on ice floats dancing
Suns overhead in tight polar circuits
Turning coronas of light without refuge
Exhausted sensation even in dark hold of ship
From nothing all day but brutal white
And when Haydon told me of this my pulse
Accelerated all my thought was on you

Voyeurism   (Chichester, January 1819)

Mysteriously into his mind after leaving Fanny
Behind in Hampstead that January there insinuates a
Grey ringdove observed from hooded covert,
Object of his feverish fantasy voyeurism—

At once shy and bold, coy, innocently knowing,
She quietly disrobes for him, pretending not
To notice he's watching from a convenient hiding
Place of artistic distance, as if behind

A false mirror—how art's a scavenger of dreams, or
How the god of love sends one one's desire
In a thin cloth shift on a chill winter night—unties
Her fine long hair, and throwing the whole wild

Lovely weight of it to one side, over her shoulder,
Loosens her bodice, unclasping her warmed jewels—
The tender taken fruits of Nature's sleepy glory
So exposed, that the pale lunar rays

Flooding through the parti-colored casements
Stain the full heavy body of their mystery
With tints of rose and gold—and by degrees
Lets her filmy underthings drift to the cold

Floor, where they pile up in a pool of fluid
Moonlight silently as seaweed gathering
Around a mermaid—the whole tableau observed
From his closet of staring awestruck wonderment—

Now the god of love will send him his desire, surely
Land him at last in his heaven where one soul

With the other mingles as the folkloric rose
Marryeth its odor with the violet—

While around the walls the detached, impassive
Carved angels press their wings into stone
And their serene lips firmly together, to keep in
All comment on the scene that's unfolding—

The girl, frisky panic-swift as a child
Leaping into icy water, dives through an amethyst
Pool of moonlight into frigid medieval sheets
Meant to close upon the hidden onlooker's

Private heaven—but which, once her formerly
Desired body is actually in between them,
Become the jaws of a predatory Nature to him,
A Gravemouth place, site of ancient buried

Memory, death breathing in the marriage bed,
The hoodwinker hoodwink'd in his own stratagem—
It is about then when as Severn notes,
The distraught look starts to come over him—

The Speechlessness of the Imagined Other

(St. Agnes' Eve, January 1819)

She comes, she comes again, sighing like a ringdove
in the pallid moonshine, or tongueless Philomel
who can not utter her ravisher's name
because he has stolen away her articulation

leaving only the unvoiced melody to swell
toward meaning in her throat and die, much as poor Tom
heart-stifled and without expression, because
though he had the pain he did not have the words,

and was otherwise more innocent than this girl,
who is only acting the part of being hoodwink'd,
is actually not sleeping or dreaming at all,
and has in mind—so Junkets has invented her—

only a love-starved poet's hungry identifying pleasure.

Returning with a sore throat from the theme-park
    medievalism
Of Stansted, cold stone, Regency Gothic, and writing
The Eve of St. Agnes on Haslam's thin genteel sheets
Of large blue paper meant for my letters to George—

To London, depression, withdrawal in Hampstead, feeling
For light and shade, finding mostly shade, opaque
Charades of passion, Brown's valentine to Fanny,
Threatening her with a whipping for being naughty,

The triangulated sexual badinage, Fanny's evasive
Flirting, and the dirty minded Brown's
Impossible possessiveness, overplaying his role
As my protector and guide, making me feel a toy,

Fanny's mother calling me a mad boy, knowing no woman
Could ever love me, holding as I do that place
Among men which among women is held by
Snub-nosed brunettes with converging eyebrows.

Disquieting and ambiguous, the snakewoman knew
How to give body to the object of a god's
Desire merely by breathing on his eyes.

Outside the gaslights of Gloucester Square went dark.
Excitement, mercurial lights on claret, fog,
The last piano note fading on warm hands.

Beneath the Aeolian harp and the caged
Parrot he thought he saw rainbow scales
Flashing, and silver moons shone blue as ice

On her glowing sweat beaded shoulders.
She breathed on his eyes like Lamia, and made
Him feel he was zoning in his nervous arms

The quicksilver motive of those fictive dreams
Where love melds into death, and vanishing
Sleep fills itself with ominous programs,

Until the street vendors came out to air their morning cries.

Cayenne   (February–March 1819)

I drank claret without restraint for six weeks
I coated my throat with pepper in order to enjoy
The claret better. My funds grew low, I felt idle, my throat
Continued to hurt. I ended my relations with Isabella

Jones. If I have ever met a woman who I really
Think would like to be married to a poem
And to be given away by a novel, it is Isabella Jones,
Of whom I have had no libidinous thought

Until provoked by her, when we drank whiskey
In her rooms, and had a curious feast.
She gave me a pheasant to take away, but to this day
I don't know who bagged whom, nor what the game.

At Brown's, Wentworth Place, Hampstead　　　　(April 1819)

3 April: Fanny B. and her family move in next door. He gives Fanny the Bright Star sonnet, reads with her the story of Paolo and Francesca in Dante: Fate fell across their love also while they too read a love tale, that of the obsessed Lancelot and "how him love thrall'd." He "kissed her mouth all trembling." That night Keats dreams of Paolo and Francesca in hell. He floats through the whirling atmosphere of hell with a beautiful figure whose lips are joined to his for what seems an age. But still they are all in hell, together, yet isolated, bound, yet still faithless, and forever alone.

Recurrence (April 1819)

She moves in next door, we huddle over
The doomed infatuated ones in Dante,
My blood over-heats, the world-wind blows,

She looks pale as Millamant the Sunday
We dine, and our fate is sealed; like a recurrence
Of fate dream, she moves in, we linger

Together over Dante, and when as not
Quite lovers we hurtle off into
The black light storm, I feel like I can't breathe;

By the end of April, wild desire's
Escaped the world, with its hundred eyes;
Ahead lies loving her, and the pale fever.

Irresolution (April 1819)

Easy and uneasy indolence, depression,
Languor, idle fevers, naps, and fretful
Declensions into uncertainty
Frustrate my efforts to get a poem started,
And then in the stifling hold of all these moods
After a disturbed night reading with Fanny
Dante's canto about Paolo and Francesca
Reading of Lancelot, and "how him love thrall'd"
I dreamed of being in that circle of sad hell
Where the enervating world-wind blew hard
Rain back into my face, as on a night borne stage
And I and a pale lady seemed to whirl
Through bleak hell space, joined at the mouth
By that word she breathed into me like a fate
I floated with, through that Melancholy Storm

La Belle Dame (A Fever Lune)   (April 1819)

A beautiful fish is flashing like an electric eel plugged into
the marshlife of some primordial littoral he hasn't yet explored
. . . and then, with cruel abrupt suddenness, he awakens. He
can never forgive his mother for dying over and over in this
dream, just as she swims back from death to him and he—Paladin,
palely loitering—is about to take her in his arms. Even inside
the dream he can sense the disappointment coming, feel the mo-
ment of sinking into a desired release again being postponed,
and energy, a swan locked in a hoop, subsiding into clammy
paralysis. The same old narrative of loss, replayed over and over
again.

The strange lassitudes, the sexual latitude of the dream. Stifling
in his night shirt, he wakes up with a slight fever, and lies awake
and depressed, shivering and with a taste of poison on his tongue.
Riverine currents of language swirl in his head, producing blurred
watercolor landscapes of symbolic revenge, of withered sedge
and lying Loreleis, lovers floating and fading—all mindless,
senseless, faithless, pointless. Images from the dream still linger,
but unformed, inchoate, like faces emerging from a pan of water
in a darkroom, then fading away. Something about her forgot-
ten smile, pale, miserable, the long curve of the lips over a mouth
unusually wide like his own—her dark head collapsed in sen-
suous exhaustion on the sweat-drenched pillow.

April 15: he goes out to Well Walk to pick up the things of Tom's
he'd left behind in fleeing the scene of his brother's terminal
agonies. He finds the packet of fake love letters written to Poor
Tom by the nonexistent Frenchwoman. Along with rage against
the hoax, there pulses through him a sick feeling of recognition:
deception and delusion, the twin assassins of innocent nature,
again enter the picture hand in hand, slipping in on the bogus

91

music of an imaginary woman's voice. His fever, his enervated tiredness, his sore throat all argue that he too has become infected, and will himself now suffer in his turn the same helpless fate, a chain victim of the perfidy of that deceptive voice.

5. Phosphorescence

The Summer Triangle   (1819)

After a night of whisk and brag and gin and water
At Rice's cardplaying club on Poland Street,
Coming out before dawn under the lyric stars,
Vega conspicuous at the point of the Lyre

At five o'clock of a summer morning encompassing
286 square degrees of the London Arabic sky,
The whole fate drama hoving into view,
While the slow making of souls overshadows

Every thing—in this vale of sorrows and of
The stubborn drive to find something outside
The frail shell of ourselves and our concerns
With which we might identify—

The burden of the mystery producing a sharp, acute
Light that pierces the drawingroom, the sparring
Ring and the cockpit footloose Junkets haunts,
Deneb and Altair locked across the dark

Sky to form the asterism known as the Summer Triangle

A Pocket Apollo   (Spring 1819)

The thrush or nightingale that began calm-throated
Lifted the curtain on a tragic play that opened
Like an evening glory, with Vega in the Summer
Triangle, poised overhead to be sung

As Aeschylus sang the god on Delos discovering
Poetry in a mimetic touching of the strings
Which serendipitously charms every thing.
That forward spring Keats stood beneath Brown's plum

Tree, head cocked alertly as the listening forest
Faun in a tragic masque strains to pick up
Distant chords unheard by the mortal players,
A modal continuum of quiet minor song

That keeps the Ring Nebula in Lyra spinning
And swimming, an incandescent sea of gas
That surrounds its central star the way grief
And lament echo and engulf suffering. Dying

Back into ambient underground rustling, then rising,
Birdsong continued to flow from the covert glade,
Drowning Brown's garden in a grief-drenched shade.
Mortality like a fist closed in Keats' throat

While the golden lyre lying at his side,
Touched by no one, tuned to no human register,
Poured out liquid notes to the unwearied underground
Ear of the alert listening forest, smooth,

Clear as claret cool out of a cell a mile
Deep. All through that aching starlit spring
In Hampstead the god kept being born
As the stunned, exhausted player was abandoned.

Digressive   (Saturday, April 11, 1819)

I strolled the Heath with gentle Coleridge
that archangel now a little damaged,
greying, shaky, wandering, rolling-eyed,
yet still air-floating, shadow-loving:
we spoke of nightingales, nymphs
who live beneath the ocean, dark,

far metaphysics, stars,
monsters, the kraken, ghost stories,
and how the mind keeps on
going, discharging into wordless
depths of feeling the wreath'd

trellis of a working brain
even when the lights are out,
the eyes are closed, and the river
of the dream starts flowing
sweet and wild and sure in language strange

Coleridge I believe was by this time changed with age to a great ruin, though I must add that he later said of me, as of this occasion, I looked dirty, and already had death in my hand.

Philomel   (Brown's Garden, Hampstead, Spring 1819)

Coleridge also heard the nightingale in Highgate
That April, a liquid note already rising in Keats' heart and
    throat
Like hawthorn and eglantine in the pastoral
Woods where ecstasy once poured forth. With the well
Tuned warble of her nightly sorrow, Philomel's
Heart having been converted into a pincushion,
The mere thought of further feeling turned
Her throat into an avenue of sweet descant.

Thus the spring of the Odes began
To stretch back to Izaak Walton and
The seventeenth century. Thus fared
The night wanderer, pulled by gravity toward Coleridge's
Garden in Highgate, where the lilac blooms,
The moon grows full, Samuel Pepys plays
His flageolet, and her elegiac lament,
Rising, catches in Keats' throat.

Gulled (May 1819)

When the American frontier adventurer and bird painter Audubon gulled my brother George into sinking his nest egg on a Mississippi steamboat, I guessed immediately that the craft would be ancient, flyblown and leaky. I knew the family money might as well have been packed up in a postal satchel, tied to a sheet anchor and dropped to the oozy greenish depths of that primal American wilderness where only evil blooms—so savage did I instantly perceive George's folly to be. Still I was not about to say anything; for my own folly in risking my existence on something as fragile and doubtful as the transcription of birdsong, at that time—feverishly writing as if to tempt fate into the onslaught of terminal illness—made all nature seem an Audubon to me.

Charles Brown and
The Nightingale Ode

In that pleasant forward spring when everything living quickleapt into sudden bloom, some bird—a thrush, or early nightingale—set up its nest in a covert of my garden, keeping Keats up late those fine nights with its tranquil and continual joy of song. One morning he took his chair from the breakfast table to the grass plot under the burgeoning plum tree, and in two or three hours there, filled with writing many scraps of paper, which upon coming in, he quietly thrust behind some books. I found them, and though the writing was not well legible, and it was difficult to make out the stanzas on so many scraps, with his help I succeeded in piecing it together.

It Is Getting Late (May 1819)

Half bottle of claret drunk alone—a soft
Dusk falls in this dragon world of men
Who cannot see what flowers are at their feet
Once the swarming of phenomena begins

Better perhaps to guess than to see
Those flowers of death's close growth and breathing,
Lustrous, fragrant, spongy, aethereal,
Shadowy thought left to supply its own

Earth-figuring text finds this evanescent
Diffuse sense efflorescing, this slow
Faint luminous phosphorescence rising
From the forever speculative ground

Phosphorescence

Beneath that darkling covert where the still
Invisible bird has built its nest in
Brown's garden like the bearer of a singing
Telegram arriving this forward spring

From a future I am not fated to be in
Life shows the magic hand of chance
At work in every little thing—not least
This tranquil song, whose joy fulfills my search

For the elegiac silver lining
Landing in my lap like this—just when my
Mind was most open to the glow that comes
Up like stardust from the things growing there

Ego Shed

The garden is deserted, the bird alone
in it, as made known by its song,
giving to that which is without language
a place in the realm of sounding
spirit, but who is listening? the
poet as silent witness over there
under his plum tree bower—his whole
being going out into the song, leaving
him reported among the missing

Brown's Garden (May 1819)

Concealed in the glade, the bird opened up again into pure,
tireless sounding—a quick series of low fluty notes, a clear long
note on one pitch then spiraling up the scale, becoming fainter
until the last long drawn out notes fade—time passing, the brevity
of life, its tenuousness, its fragility—it begins to grow dark, today
also is over—

6. Sweet Surrender

Indolence

Fanny only a cry away, but correctness compels distance
Being in uncertainty, sitting here under Brown's plum tree
From which the falling leaves waft or flutter two or
Three hours of the morning, back again in the afternoon
The sky swells with clouds, yet no shower falls till once
The hero has raised himself from his bed of flowery
Grass, where, dieted with poetry and the faint praise
Of coming times which may or may not be so disinterested,
    he
Remains ineligible for marriage because too indolent to make
    a living.

Inanition

Cash stock too low to hire a coach to go
Out to visit my sister in Walthamstow,
How can I afford to even think of nuptials?
Willing to sink into insensitivity,
A wasp caught in honey, I drown my
Sting in the indolent pleasure of a
Warm season spent too close to you to be
Able to pull myself together, make money
And become eligible to marry.

Psyche's Bower

All but flesh dissolving in her moist bud,
The wishword of opening blossoms less rich,
Sweet tartness of the freckle-pink shrine,
Sanctuary of blissful stasis, hushed cache
Of blue-white and silver star flowers,
Million pleasures of her white breasts,
All the soft roundness of the growing
Peach on the too high branch, still out of reach
Though I am forever stretching out my hand.

First Person

You swear I'm the first to love you but I know
The princess in the legend does not fall
Into just any arms, nor does the first person
Who walks over the mountain into the

Kingdom necessarily get to be its prince;
When I say you are as beautiful yet not
So talismanic as that enchanting lady
Who drops men out of paradise for

So little as one blink of a sleepy eye
Please don't think I'm being melancholy,
Fanny; when I say "I" it isn't *I* I mean
But a stubborn presence who keeps coming

In and filling up the story, turning heads,
Drawing attention one more time to
This idle, empty scarecrow figure
When I know all eyes ought to be on you.

Sweet Surrender (Summer 1819)

Even in thought to burst, Mistress Melancholy Storm,
My tongue like your grape upon my palate, warm
Bosom rising with each tender taken breath,
Weds your loveliness with the hour of my death.

Yet sweet surrender tastes like poison in my mouth. Your
Sex and my death obsess me, a hushed cottony
Sheath of feeling in which I hang through long summer
Days like some unborn thing in its larval sac, suspended.

My jealousy turning churlish in my exile
From your willfulness, no officer in yawning quarters
Or swain in pastoral shade, I cannot live on water
Grass and smiles while you attend dances with cadets.

Who Is La Belle Dame and Why Am I   (1819)
Going on Like This Anyway?

Warning, betrayal and death; deep disquiet,
self disgust. The Paladins of old who lived
upon water grass and smiles for years together
wandered too close to the fatal

sedge of the sexual, and were consumed
with a feverish light in their dazed eyes,
they tumbled from their horses into a sensual
melancholy, or gordian complication

of feelings, ending up in strangulation.
I turn to Burton, vehement in my confused
misogyny, marking up the *Anatomy*
of Melancholy with vengeful comments.

I have not a right feeling towards women.
I think insults in a lady's company.
I have infinite misgivings about their motives.
What does their interest in me really mean.

The Anatomy of Melancholy   (Summer 1819)

Love, universally defined to be *desire*—here
The old philosopher hits the plague spot,
The itch of the sexual which there is no scratching
Without visions, fever, bondage, evaporation
Of the loved one just at the point of realization
Of the promised and indefinitely postponed feast,
She having turned out a lamia in her fixation
On the deceptions of the sexual chase, her bait
Desire, Myself the hunted one, consoled
And shattered by the double revelation
She is an illusion, not a vampire or a woman after all.

Collaborators (to Fanny B.)   (Summer 1819)

Deathlike in my trances, filled with macabre dreams, I kill off
the heroine in our tragedy while Brown runs around town with
female merchants of the pleasure trade. We are supposed to be
writing for money and I find this gives me a great contempt for
the public and for myself. Still I am filling up paper at a great
pace. Brown's schemes for grotesque turns in the story, lurid
lights and constant access of the passions inflame me with private
questionings when I think of the liberty with which he behaves
toward you. Of all my tragedies you may be the symbolic heroine.
Still I remain irritated, riddled, withdrawing, identifying love and
death in the biological process of my dream lover who returns
to her vampire state just as my prince is about to take her. This
is a thing I have long brooded upon. She goes up in smoke and
this may be my symbolic revenge. Nine hundred lines of *Lamia*
and act one of our tragedy under my belt. Brown insists we are
to become rich. I feel only a withered, drowsy numbness when
the work stops, and a sense I will die of these writing fevers one
day, if my irrational love for you does not overcome me first.

7. A Warm Situation

Love is in bondage to death and oblivious
A woman with wild hair, enmeshed in dream,
Cries out in the archaic Saxon dusk,
And I can feel the self shrinking from here

As the blue cloud floats out over the dune
Like a heavy dream, under a moon that
Appears pitted and gibbous as it catches
The cold spray of desire in its light nets

Weight   (Winchester, September 1819)

After another fine sharp temperate night
It is a warm morning. This is part of the world.
Summer light and dust blow yellow
Filmed clouds into the air. The brown stubble

Fields feel warm, give off a red excited
Glow like irritated raspberry marks
On fair skin, with its soft white weight,
As the doleful choir of gnats still wails,

And the maiden at the manor window shakes
The sheets out, or is it her fine light hair
That flows or is flung from the storybook casement,
That causes me to stop to catch my breath?

Lost Horizons (September 1819)

To slip the cold grasp of a familiar ghost
Who presses a finger on those quick streams
That pulse beside the throat, and makes each breath
A knife of ice, I climb the mystery steps
To reach the altar of the shrine of archaic
Sacrifice, where the veiled priestess I find
So spooks me my heart's too small to hold
Its blood, then parts her veils and lets me
Penetrate beyond the lily and the snow
To where I must not think, because I beam
In blank splendor as a mild comfort moon
Rising above the wide water meadows
Chills yet consoles me, and the great work
Of accepting life now can be begun.

The Fall of Hyperion   (Fall 1819)

Turning from the small inlet to uncharted waters
he plunged again into *Hyperion*, a salvage operation
designed to pull guesses at heaven from
the submerged locker of his curious mind,

but poetry can't tell its dreams, and when
the filmed clouds reel slowly back
into the projector, overhead the whole
dark planetarium's suddenly lit up with stars.

A Warm Situation   (Winchester 1819)

I surprise myself by how much pleasure I live alone in. Fields where a month ago men bound up their wheat all day, and the harvesters, leaning on their instruments like flagging vines, complained of heat, while hirundines passed across the sky in great assemblies, are now a brown stubble under mist in a cool blue dusk, with sweet moon light all around, while stone-curlews cry late into the fine sharp starlight-tempered evenings.

Hop-picking goes on without interruption, as it continues warm. The whole air of the villages of an evening is perfumed by effluvia from the hops drying in the kilns. Is it this aromatic resonance that makes my brain feel pleasantly drowsy when I am on my walks, or when I am alone composing? Night dews, days calm and cloudless. I am most happy when I am alone and not myself, far from home and in a warm situation. The farm women gather in the pear-mains, golden rennets, and golden pippins. Sweet days, golden eves, red horizons. Just at the close of day several teams of ducks fly over the cathedral fronts from the forest, headed off probably to find a congenial stream. My chance of immortality is to learn the tune of nature's quiet power, and take up my lyre, a pocket Apollo as Mrs. Jones teased me once, assimilated completely to that calm song.

Blowing weather, the walks begin to be strewn with leaves, grass now grows on them very fast. No fruit left for the few remaining wasps, and the tops of the beeches begin to be tinged with yellow hue. What is it that wants only our rich dying to bring it to perfection?

Growth   (September 1819)

To rescue into consciousness one fact
I never liked a stubble field so much as now
Guesses at heaven, memories swerving back
From the heart's desire to a negated landscape,
Detour into self's uneasy past,

Nervous resonances heard in the humble
Mossed cottages of the rustic villages
Through which, like a shade of Bonaparte's army,
The grand dusty march of intellect passes
Scorching the earth behind it with understanding

The brown granary in my blood turns gold
The cells of the heavy beehive are brimming
Yet down inside the warm breathing of things
Growth is still mysteriously going on
Deceived into thinking summer won't end

Autumn (Winchester, 1819)

In that last calm, fine temperate season before
First chill, I wanted to compose without this fever.
The air had a sharpness that kept my blood warm.
On the night coach back from London, I resolved
For books, fruit, French wine, and a little fine
Music out of doors—like Mr. Pepys, who said
He liked to play his flageolet in his garden
A little, on nights when the moon shone full.
Or to loll on a lawn by some old dark water
Lillied pond, eat white currants and see gold
Fish, or go to the fair if I am good—and feel
How a stubbled plain brushed by a calm looks warm.

Laudanum

When to relieve this anxious binding tightness
Within my chest, I drown two or three cloudy
Drops of laudanum in a cool glass of claret
And invoke Lethe with its autumnal mists,

Time slows, and I hear a mournful choir
Of bugs born this morning among the river
Shallows only to die before evening,
Sinking as the late light lives and dies,

While drawing downward gravity grows jealous
When wings of closure flutter over us
Beating as if impatient for history to take place,
And gathering darkness swallows up the sky.

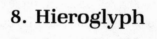

8. Hieroglyph

Three Days' Dream   (October 15–17, 1819)
(Weekend at Brawnes')

Back in London objectless, unemployed
I walk the streets in an abstract state
Till like Orpheus in hell I look back
At my lone star fixed in splendor, high above
The scene an unseen hand determines
Her mother will take me in for a long
Weekend that makes my senses spin, puts warm
Love in my arms and leaves me with this
Terrible feeling I must soon dissolve
Into thin air even before death's anthems
Are chanted, or time hangs its cloudy trophies
Waking from this three days' dream I know a man
In love cuts the sorriest of figures
Yet still cry to dream again like Caliban

Engagement

There is something about this time of year,
When the light gets thin and seems to hold
Within itself the fading hue of a sky
From which all color is slowly dissolving,

That brings back old lunes, and weeds of mourning
Hung in secret lockers are unstored to air,
Radiating old anguish all around,
While nights turn chill, and sacrificial

Steams rise from thatch eaves in pale sunrise thaws,
Vapors streaming heavenward like ghosts
As I leave you, elated yet uneasy in
The lightheadedness that sweeps over me—

Having given you the garnet ring, yet
Bound to draw back, knowing that there being
No hope of losing what is adamantine
Is exactly the problem with this bond.

Wasted Winter

You dazzled me, I have this feeling I'm dissolving
in your wretched thrall, I can't breathe
when I see you, when I don't see you, I can't stand it
when anyone looks at you or speaks to you,
I'm afraid my rivals with their greedy eyes
will lap up my feast before I ever have
my chance to partake of it, I find the
thought of these dances you go to dangerous,
like swimming among submerged reefs,
my mouth fills up with a familiar poison
taste, when shall we pass a day alone,
where shall I learn to get my peace again

I can't stand the echoes of that
orchestra when I can't dance
with you myself, I dwindle,
I feel confused, I feel distracted,
I feel unfairly treated by my fate,
I feel a nervous tightness in my throat
and chest, I am tired of feeling,
it grows cold, snow has fallen,
I don't feel like going out,
I am listless in my writing,
I don't feel like picking up my pen,
I shall publish nothing I have written,
let the lovers of my poetry find their
way into each other's arms if I may not.

In the Chill, Bustling Dusk of Early Winter

Passing tradesmen in the labyrinth of mean streets and lodging houses around Cheapside tucked their heads into their coats and plowed through the crowd of street vendors hawking hot eels, hot pea soup and doubtful pies. Bow bells rang out five as Keats idly drifted in a fever daydream, wandering past the counting houses and companies. It was the time when wholesale houses closed their shutters with a moody sense of wealth, but retail dealers, still diligent, turned up the gas that was conveyed in little soldered pipes. As it flared up in many a brilliant form, Keats— to whose exhausted eyes everything seemed watery, floating, tinged with memory overlays of roaming these same narrow, darkening lanes with his brothers, as if in another life—remarked once again on the beauty of the world. Despite the well-advertised health dangers of its fumes, he could not help delighting in the way gaslight conjured out of the gloom of the city night a scene as laden with the swimming forms of fable as those of Ovid, Spenser or Dante, with its divine snowfall sifting like glittering dusk through the stars.

Hieroglyph

At Pond Street the lamps spun more wildly than
Two glasses of claret should have made them
The next thing I knew I was coughing in my bed
I had Brown bring the candle upstairs

I knew what to think of that vivid red drop
Produced by the erosion of an arterial wall
It was a familiar hieroglyph of fate
I've seen inscribed on several pillowcases

Like our family heraldry on a crest
All those years I've struggled to forget
But later when the blood poured out importunate
All I could say to Brown was this is unfortunate

Alone   (Wesleyan Place, May 1820)

The more she runs around to parties, the more time I spend alone in my dull rooms in Kentish Town, the lower my health grows, the deeper my moods sink, till I am in a state to envy street Scavengers and Cinder-sifters, Lumpers and Ballast-heavers, Coal-heavers, or even those Mudlarks who comb the City sewers for any scrap of stuff they can find to sell—all intent to get themselves a cup of grog, a bowl of hot pea soup or a hot eel fried in its own grease—at least they can enjoy their simple pleasures without being possessed by the Image of Laughter passing across her lips for the diversion of others.

Submarine Resurrection   (June 1820)

In a dream which I had more than once during that time, I
was locked up in a Guy's that was under the ocean. All the
doctors and students and patients were gone, but the corridors
were jammed with cadavers. The dissecting room was over-
crowded with them, all in a decomposing state, gray and clayey
of face, not yet waxed and still covered with the filthy greenish
river mud that had been upon them when the graves men
fished them out. I couldn't breathe properly and was stifled
by a hand that closed over my mouth, causing it to fill up with
fluid. Waking in a shaky sweat, I recalled the foul water that
still oozed out of the corpses when we opened them up to under-
take our anatomical studies. Often their mouths were full of
water.

The morning of the twenty-second of June I went to catch the
coach to town, but came back stunned, having again spat blood.
Till tea time I lay alone in my room, my mind tossed and twisted
by this latest dogleg of my fate. Then, though feeling somewhat
giddy and faint, and no doubt appearing pale as my own ghost,
I went off to Hunt's.

At Hunt's, Maria Gisborne, a friend of Shelley's from Italy, spoke
of breath control in opera singing, and of a famous Italian tenor,
who could by many imperceptibly small gulpings of oxygen hold
a single note seemingly indefinitely. In the best voice I could
muster at the moment, I remarked how painful that prolonged
note must be to hear, as when a diver descends too deep and
you fear he may not come up again.

Following the profound hemorrhage of later that night, with the
rupturing of a vessel, I was able to hold out alone no longer, and
had to let them move me to Hunt's hot noisy squeeze box of a

138

house—where beneath the gasping casement, like marine predators, the eel vendors, ballad singers, and resurrection men cruised dusty, glaring streets. I thought more than once then of London as Atlantis, that sunken city of the dead.

Wine and Fever   (Summer 1820)

I am in my altitudes
    after two glasses of claret
but then my diagnosis sinks
    in all over again—I feel

my lunes are sneaking up—
    I am beat all hollow—
fate goes against my pluck—
    I wanted to be great

now there's no world left me
    to be great in—anyway
I'm long since departed,
    no longer speaking from myself

but from some other being
    in whose soul I now live—
poetry information, primitive
    sense—what I can't finish

I won't begin—my doctors say
    be moderate—if they only knew
I drink out of the bottle
    till the island comes into view

9. Misfortunes

Fate Taint

Bad blood in the Keats family, showing
Itself in young John's contrary temper
Moved Abbey to sequester John's sister Fanny
A petit bourgeois fear of contamination
That may have prolonged her life, saving her
As George was saved by going off to
America, from close contact with the
Successively fading remaining brothers
A fatal susceptibility
Having been passed down in the blood stock
To drop on their mother, her brother, and God
Knows how many prior generations
An unwanted dark knowledge of how
Youth grows pale and spectre thin and dies

Devastated Angels   (Summer 1820)

His endless suspicions and moods, as though everything
He had were about to be taken from him. And it was.

Estranged from his would-be paramour, trusting no one,
His fevers exacerbated in the dog days

Of that hot dusty summer, as the vessel walls slowly gave out,
Emaciated, sad, irritated by his sister's

News about the possible perfidy of their guardian Abbey,
By Fanny Brawne, by Brown, by his brother George,

By the painful, abnormal pounding of his heart,
Going out to the Kentish Town coach stop,

He ignored its beating much too hard against his chest
But did not catch the coach into the city

Because the blood was coming up into his mouth.
Then they removed him from the darkening jealousy

Of his rooms, moved him around the corner to
Hunt's latest harried haven on Mortimer Terrace.

Hunt had money woes and migraines of his own.
The sun shone down on their dusty journalism, two

Devastated angels, one knocked out, one still flapping,
Unhappy in Hunt's crowded noisy house.

Mortimer Terrace   (Summer 1820)

In the street, Keats saw a little girl standing with one hand
Raised up over her forehead to block out the glancing sun.

He flashed back to the image of his sister Fanny—
At a comparable age—and of the pond and

Moist marshy microworlds in which they'd all bathed
And played through an age of forlorn summer

Days, in Edmonton, during his mother's
Prolonged disappearance. Never really had a mother,

The plain sense of it had sunk in during her absence,
Never known any real happiness since—

And Hunt, sympathetic as always, and sensitive
Also to the grief of his fate at least this once,

Wrote, "the apothecary's apprentice,
With a bitterness beyond aloes, thinks of the pond

He used to bathe in at school."

He summoned back the little Dante with the Bright Star
Sonnet in Fanny Brawne's handwriting, from Kentish Town,

And sent it on to her with bitter jealousy unabated,
Pre-visioning her at the convivial military balls

And gentleman's dances of a horrid future in which he'd
Take only this helpless premonitory

Role, foreseeing but unable to avert
The destruction of all his hopes. In a

Note, he told her he was sickened
"At the brute world which you are smiling with."

"Hamlet's heart was full of such misery as mine."
The lost lover, causing misery, was Ophelia.

But through the tangled hair of the drowned girl floating in water,
An image appeared suddenly clear out of the sedge-choked

Trellises of his working brain in fever, the visage of the
Perfidious queen his mother, fallen, with moisture

Darkened brow and passages of loose auburn
Hair trailing across the drenched beloved oval of the forever

Vanished face.

Misfortunes (1820)

My love for my brothers from the early loss of our parents and even earlier Misfortunes has grown into an affection "passing the Love of Women." That's why when I went back to Well Walk I broke down at the end of the street, sobbing into a handkerchief for lack of spirit to look again upon the house where Poor Tom died. I felt as though for my whole life I had been mourning someone, which was a sad thought put into my heart by my Friends—looking upon me as though they felt I ought to be in Mourning for myself—and at that moment I understood for the first time my mother's wish to be out of mourning after my father died—and within two months she took up with that miserable fellow Rawlings—a conniving clerk whose true trade it was to prey on widows—in her wretchedness she was to be forgiven—I now see that in the extremity of this existence any poor object to take one out of the world for so much as a moment, is to be desired—for anything to forget one's losses, any drug or disgrace to numb this pain—

Teru, teru. Mimetic—liquid and musical as the words
Well Walk, where he wandered with Hunt, saw
Poor Tom's ghost, broke down, that last awful
Suffocating August—it is the wounding of Philomel
That produced the lyric, a wild quiet echoing
Of mortal tribulation that drowns in
The singer's voice, as the singer dies and
The pain that drives expression is extinguished
With the sudden curtailing of the song.

I am certain he has some spell that attaches them
To him, observed Fanny Brawne of the intense
Emotionality of Keats' friends' goodbyes.
The fussing over practicalities, guilty self-
Justifying and sentimental evasions
At last set aside, their hearts got caught
In their throats' cordage by London dock,
As he got ready to board the boat that
Would take him off to that classic land to die.

Haydon, demonstrating characteristic pettiness, lack of perspective and poor timing, asks to have back some books loaned years earlier, in much happier days. And Haydon still owes him money. Shelley writes offering to pick him up at Leghorn and take him back to Pisa, but makes condescending comments about *Endymion.* A note written to him at Hunt's by Fanny is opened and read by a servant girl, who half-maliciously delays its delivery. One annoyance too many, and he breaks down and weeps for hours. Then he sets out on foot for Hampstead, dragging himself like dead weight trundled by resurrection men. He goes to Well Walk, and is seen at the end of the road on which Poor Tom had passed away, sobbing into a handkerchief. "I think there is a core of disease in me not easy to pull out," he writes Brown, who then declines to accompany him to Rome in his last days.

Suspicion (1820)

They speak of me as one would speak of a problematic child.
This is the sort of insult that only comes to men who are short—
it's hard to be a poet when you're not six feet and a lord. Don't
they know I guess what they say when I am absent? People won't
admit to me what I know in my heart with an ache like that of
a wound, that my illness is in my lung. Fanny smiles at everyone.
My brother George has cheated me out of money to throw away
on Audubon's leaky steamboats. My doctors take away my food
and blood, and my friends consign me to Italy to die without
their having to feel it too much.

Collaborators (II) (1820)

As if behind my back love and poetry conspired against me—
and fate as well by making me small—hard to be a poet when
you are not six feet and a lord—and now here's my friend Brown
doing me to death by inches with his indecent flirtations with
my Muse and with Fanny Brawne—I think henceforth I shall trust
no one—but not even by that resolution shall I ever grow tall—

Who Am I to Tell Shelley   (Summer 1820)

Tumbling down to my own incautious fathom of loss
Who am I to tell Shelley not to go near the water?
Shelley, with his long legs and pedigree, has always patronized
     me.
With nowhere better than a rented room to die in

Who am I to tell Shelley I won't be staying over?
My mind scattered by fever like a pack of cards
Who am I to tell Shelley to load every rift with ore?
Who am I to tell Shelley with my crystal ball

He will invite Leigh Hunt when I decline to join him
And on meeting Hunt's boat in Leghorn he will die at sea.
Who am I to tell Shelley he will outlive me
Not in eternity as he thought but by a matter of months.

Resolution (1820)

Seeing his friends' minds were made up
He squared his shoulders and obediently
Marched off to Italy
As if he were an infantryman going (he said)
Out to face one last artillery barrage
From the French battery—while secretly
Suspecting that the real foe was on his own side

10. Unstrung

Percipience

The last chapter starts that March, with the palpitations
That usher the naked heartache, the wound grief
Into the increasingly complex song—elegiac,
Then lyric, this liquid wounding rising in the voice
As it issues out of the quiet covert of the glade

Like bubbles rising in some clear sparkling wine
Shot through with morphine, shading violet to green,
Cool slipstream currents—Styx, Lethe—the *Maria
Crowther* becalmed in Portsmouth Roads, where
He writes of a sense of darkness coming over him—

Then comes the slow departure of the death ship,
Seasickness, panic in a cramped berth,
Foul winds, stale air, squalid dead end passage
Of ten days' quarantine in the Bay of Naples,
Five hemorrhages in nine days of a nightmare

December in Rome, pathos, delirium,
Growing conviction the whole grotesque
Adventure's being authored by a malicious
Hand—hapless history, disenchanted
Percipience of a common fate—

Mythology

As when heartache pierces the wounded throat
Of the nightingale with liquid song,
Suffering excuses itself to history
By turning loss into a symbol of feeling,
A hacking cough into a resigned sigh.
Wandering with his soul on the English shore,
Staying for waftage like Troilus betrayed
In the ancient story, Keats continued to woo
The immortals though his own mortality closed,
Torn by this unfortunate commitment
To song, and fatally dismembered
For the love of one lost girl, like Orpheus
After he didn't look back with sufficient
Alacrity at the dead mythology gaining on him.

The Spell   (Late 1820)

Wounded by a thorn, tongue cut out to keep
from uttering the lover's name—the song of the dying
bird, rising and falling, has the clarity of
pain, also the wild turbulence, the derangement. I hate

men and women more, he wrote Fanny B. in August
in his last letter before boarding the death ship: I see nothing
but thorns for the future. His friends sealed his fate
with the well-intentioned exile to Italy

on the eve of which the humiliations multiplied.
There was Shelley's patronizing invitation,
Brown's failure to accompany him, Hunt's sentimentalism,
Haydon's cruel scorn, Reynolds' envious drollery,

Bailey's parsonizing, Taylor's anxiety over business details.
But even after the ship sailed, the spell still held, no
one could breathe without thinking of him, everyone nervously
awaiting word from Severn whether or not he was still
        breathing.

Calm Evening on Shipboard   (September 1820)

Twilight, a few white clouds about and a few stars blinking—
Vega in the Summer Triangle appears to strum an unstrung lyre
like the one on the letter seal given me by Fanny Brawne on a
fine cold Christmas day in Hampstead that now seems farther
away than another Planet from the sad one I inhabit at this
moment—the waters ebbing and the Horizon a Mystery, the sea
surface calm and strange fish circling below in green and violet
shallows at the turning of the tide—a sense of a kind of quiet
growth of darkness in the deeper, outer channels—with my last
English evening coming on.

En Route
(Aboard the *Maria Crowther*, September 1820)

Woodhouse, Haslam, Taylor came aboard with us
Then left the boat at Gravesend waving goodbyes.
Directed by the eyes of others
To look into myself, I find fear closing,
In the long rush of fever storms, on the end
That will fulfill all these frightful thoughts
By permanently smothering feeling.
In the green distance the open sea reflects
A black fate wedged against a flame gray sky.

Melancholy Watch, (September 1820)
the Downs

My melancholy watch, mid-quarter-deck,
Drifting: I follow the play of the gulls.
The sun is long gone down, the east darkling,
The ship drifts. In the west, some brightness remains.
Momently there are two flights of gulls moving
One to the east into the dark and one
Out of the west, in the last rays of the sun,
Left and right so entirely dissimilar
That the name gull quite falls from them
As I watch, and the chiaroscuro
Of the evening is torn open, altering
Everything: so that now everything is
Only itself: the gulls, myself closer
In nature than if I still knew their name,
Yet at the same time moving farther out,
Sinking deeper into a fading sky
Which soaks them up like ink accepting water,
Coaxing darkness out of reluctant night,
Bringing on the abolition of that false
Identity which made naming possible.

Gravesend   (September 1820)

Severn visited the chemist for laudanum at Gravesend,
Sent to buy cold solace in a bottle for Keats.
They were becalmed. He fell into frequent fevers.
Slowly they drifted past light airs bright towns
Again, the death boat held in doubtful suspension
Like opium in alcohol. Listless passage
Toward awareness' blockaded harbor,
Temptation to lose control, go overboard,
Desperate awareness of his love situation
In which the very thing which he wants
To live for the most will be his death's occasion
And yet he cannot help it. Who can help it?

False Confidences at Sea

The second day out, at Gravesend, a pretty young female consumptive passenger, also bound for Italy, came on board, and joined their little English traveling party. She was just Fanny Brawne's age, and just as obviously as Keats himself, not long for this world. Looking upon her with a haunted fascination as if looking into a mirror, he talked himself into exhaustion that second night at sea for her benefit and his own as well—and to Severn, later in their cabin, confided she appeared to be at a more advanced stage of wasting than himself; as identically in her turn did the female passenger, Miss Cotterell, when for a moment they were alone together on deck, confide to Severn that poor sad Keats' state seemed to her much more pitiable than her own.

But following these alternating empty confidences, both desperately self-deceived invalids were constantly sick on the high seas, Miss Cotterell fainting like clockwork when the portholes of their common cabin were left shut, Keats swept by gales of coughing when they were left open—as if their respective morbidities were in syzygy—and Severn remembers Keats' face never lost that starved haunted expression after this time.

Naples   (October–November 1820)
(The Quarantine)

Eternally vanishing now perhaps for ever in humiliation
and ill health, three weeks' voyaging, more hemorrhages
that stained the Mediterranean a deeper wine dark hue
of depression, he planned to kill the monotony
of his agony during the days of the quarantine
when his final formal love cry to Fanny Brawne
was sent from the hideous closed cabin
with laudanum, but Severn kept the bottle from his hands.

Traveling on their interminable stagecoach through the bleak wastelands of the Campagna, the bone-weary Englishmen saw scabrous herdsmen poking at the skulls of horses, starved dogs scavenging in broken-down drainage canals, and rotting body parts of bandits impaled on poles. Fetid swamp air and vapors wreathed the countryside in suffocating morning mists which suddenly gave way to a high noon of brutal, relentless sun. The towns were malaria-infected: Keats' hacking cough echoed through a flyblown trattoria where a crone in a black shawl served them a cadaverous duck. Severn tasted shot in it; Keats contended it was a decoy. The cardinal hunting with a gun on the road to Rome—they met him late that afternoon, just as Keats began to be unable to differentiate the objects of his vision from purely subjective phenomena—had an owl with a mirror fastened to its breast feathers. The owl was tied to a long stick, which the red-cloaked cardinal had set up to attract passing songbirds. Seeing their own images, the birds approached, and the cardinal fired errantly at them. Severn felt pity for the owl, which had by far the best chance of being shot, and Keats a curious sense of identification.

Progress of the Colors of the Sky   (Rome, November 1820)

Black the hue of mourning robes still drapes the air
Over the Spanish Steps, till dawn slips on marble
Lions aboard Bernini's broken boat
A white of cloth they wrap the dead in;
Through this pallor a pink of conch shells seeps,
Then blue flames consume the whole of heaven.

Noon blasted by bolts of brass and gold
Steeps my brain in a dreamful fever-sleep
Wherein I labor beating out the links
Of fate, link after link, an endless chain
Of sorrows and sweats and nervous tossings.
When I have strength to prop myself up

Beside the window next, the air appears as
Corporeal tissue decomposing, like
Dusty carcasses of animals that hang
A week at market, darkening by degrees
From a faded terracotta red—the color
Of the roofs of Rome still saturated

With the sun's warmth as the dying day cools
The pope's dome to a dark grape in lemon dusk
And with twilight one star lifts itself above
The city, pauses and plunges downward—
Into an overflowing well of
Violet, the shade of separation.

Unstrung

His lyre pulled down from the sky, stomped on, broken—Even
with Socrates to be dosed with hemlock so a drowsy numbness
might dissolve his sense while self was jettisoned into the winds
of space—Even this relief was denied him, in Rome, when Severn
hid the laudanum—The kind but uncomprehending Severn hard-
ly knew him any more—It was easier to assume his mind was
gone than to face the vision of the black winds of the negative
universe that was painted on his face—

Sidereal Study—Above the Spanish Steps   (December 1820)

Hearing Severn play piano arrangements of Mozart
Sympathies in their room of lament and quarantine,

In pain, needing to hitch a ride to the stars,
But knowing all that instant information (primitive sense)

Required to throw a leg over the little horse
Is a mode to which he is now forever denied access,

Equuleus setting in glory overhead as he peers
Into the nascent no moon dark above the Spanish Steps

Second Thoughts (Rome, 1821)

I should have had her in health I would have remained well.

Sentiment II (Fanny Brawne)

His fevers as he spoke of his writing times were I believe what killed him—and before the end there was the terrible time of tears and pains, in which we did come to know each other somewhat after all, yet never again so happily as on that Christmas Day—and from Italy he sealed his last letters with that same Tassie seal—and when it came at last time for him to design a gravestone for himself, a duty that would bring few persons to think of poetry or art, he ordered Severn to have carved a Greek lyre with half its strings broken—to show his classical genius cut off before its maturity, Severn supposed—but Severn never knew—and beneath it, he instructed Severn to have carved the legend Here Lies One Whose Name Was Writ In Water— ever a man for fine sentiment was Mr. Keats—

English Cemetery, Rome   (1821)

Heap turfs of daisies on my
pretty pagan grave,
beneath the pyramid's
restless eye—
and say if with thy
crystal conscience thou
wouldst not wish thine
own heart dry
of blood—so in my
veins red life
might stream again—

Combustion   (Rome, 1821)

His having died of consumption
every thing he had touched in his
final fever, every stick of furniture
in every room in which he'd been,
the wallpaper he had looked upon,
the bed in which he'd lain dying,
the chairs on which he'd sat,
had to be stripped down,
dismantled, put to the flames

Coda: Echo and Variation

"The calculable law of tragedy"
—Hölderlin

I

Mariners don't think too much about the deeps
Of the Other at the bottom of the ocean.
Like a sort of north star which in shining
Accelerates all my thought from far off,

Identity presses on me so all day
As to tease sleep out of my anxious mind.
Melancholy lunes, identifying with
Tom dismal and forlorn and spitting blood.

Heart, ever out of its element, keeps
Identifying with Hamlet, a dying
Sun beats down, the confused heifer lows,
Feeling nature's mass fall and spill like

A blade. Light plays cleanly upon bronze.
Above the victim's head the priest suspends
Our fear of death. And this abandoned town—
Where love melds into death, and vanishing

Sleep fills itself with ominous programs,
The whole fate drama hoving into view
Before dawn under the lyric stars—
Tacks around the cove and disappears.

A boat tacks around the cove and disappears
From the world on paper liberty wings.
At five o'clock of a summer morning
Sleep fills itself with ominous programs,

The whole fate drama hoving into view
Before dawn under the lyric stars.
She comes, she comes again, sighing like
Poetry and not any woman

I've floated with, through that melancholy
Marshlife of some primordial littoral
Where love melds into death, and vanishing
Riverine currents of language swirl

Like death on my tongue poisonous as
That word she breathes into me like a fate.

III

As time washes round these human shores
It must be poisonous to life itself,
The stubborn desire to find something outside
The perfidy of that deceptive voice.

Identity presses on me so all day
I'm obliged to go out, and when I come in
To somewhere even more crazy and strange
I plunge into abstract images to ease

Being in that circle of sad hell
Nature normally holds off from us.
A strange adolescent beside her strange body,
I can never forgive my mother for dying.

But everything's explained in advance,
What's planned falls away before what happens.

The same old narrative of loss replayed
On her glowing sweat beaded shoulders,
The night wanderer pulled by gravity
Sinking into a desired release again.

Outside the gaslights of Gloucester Square went dark,
Street vendors came out to air their morning cries.
I and a pale lady seemed to swirl
Through hell space, joined at the mouth

While the slow making of souls overshadows
Every thing in this vale of sorrows—
Lovers floating and fading, all mindless,
Assassins of innocent nature—

My blood over-heats, the world-wind blows,
I must write to chase them from my mind.

V

She moves in next door, we huddle over
Paolo and Francesca in Dante: Fate
Floats through the whirling atmosphere
Of the sexual, and is consumed

While in Hampstead the god keeps being born;
Sweet surrender tastes like poison in my mouth,
My blood over-heats, the world-wind blows
Every thing in this vale of sorrows

Through the whirling atmosphere of hell
To London, depression, withdrawal—
Warning, betrayal and death deep
At work in every little thing—seeing

London as Atlantis, that sunken city
Sifting like glittering dust through the stars.

VI

The moving waters at their priestlike task,
Polaris growing bright against the sky
Like an evening glory, with Vega
Swimming, an incandescent sea of gas

That surrounds its central star the way
A modal continuum of quiet
Keeps the Ring Nebula in Lyra spinning,
Show the magic of chance at work:

She moves in next door, we huddle over
The doomed infatuated ones in Dante,
The burden of the mystery producing
A mimetic touching of the strings

With which we might identify
Deneb and Altair locked across the dark.

VII

The night wanderer's pulled by gravity
Through hell with a beautiful figure whose lips,
Those flowers of death's close growth and breathing,
Glow like irritated raspberry marks
Once the swarming of phenomena begins.

The story of Paolo and Francesca
So spooks me my heart's too small to hold
The elegiac silver lining
Once the swarming of phenomena begins
To wed your loveliness with the hour of my death.

We dine, and our fate is sealed. Like a recurrence
The doomed infatuated ones in Dante
Who cannot see what flowers are at their feet
Once the swarming of phenomena begins
Cry out into the archaic Saxon dusk

Where ecstasy once poured forth, with
Shadowy thought left to supply its own
Sheath of feeling in which I hang all through
That aching starlit spring in Hampstead,
Once the swarming of phenomena begins.

VIII

When I say "I" it isn't *I* I mean,
This idle, empty scarecrow figure,
Unborn thing in its larval sac suspended,
Though I am forever stretching out my hand

When I know all thoughts ought to be on you—
Better perhaps to guess than to see
Poetry in a mimetic touching of
A future I am not fated to be in—

The brevity of life, its tenuousness—
Faint luminous phosphorescence, rising
Desire—myself the hunted one consoled—
To slip the grasp of a familiar ghost

Causes me to stop and catch my breath,
Happy when I am alone and not myself.

Blue dusk, with sweet moon light all around.
As the blue cloud floats out over the dune
The doleful choir of gnats still wails.
Riverine currents of language swirl.

A woman with wild hair enmeshed in dream
Cries out into the archaic Saxon dusk—
Clear long note on one pitch then spiraling up
Just as my prince is about to take her.

The submerged locker of his curious mind
Is a thing I have long brooded upon.
Love and death in the biological
Secret lockers are unstored to air.

The biological process of my dream
So spooks me my heart's too small to hold
The cold spray of desire in its light nets,
And the woman at the manor window shakes

The sheets out—or is it her fine light hair?—
Like a heavy dream, under a moon that
Appears pitted and gibbous as it catches
The quicksilver motive of my fictive dreams

With tints of blue and gold; and by degrees
Riverine currents of language swirl
Through the blue cloud that floats out over the dune
In bondage to death and oblivious

Blue dusk, with sweet moon light all around.

X

While nights turn chill, and sacrificial
Vapors streaming heavenward like ghosts
Rising above the wide water meadows
Pass across the sky in great assemblies,

Time slows, and I hear a mournful choir
Invoke Lethe with its autumn mists
While hirundines pass across the sky,
Deceived into thinking summer won't end.

But poetry can't tell its dreams, and when
Ducks fly over the cathedral fronts
The harvesters, leaning on their instruments,
Loll on a lawn by some old dark water,

Assimilated completely to that calm
Down inside the warm breathing of things.

XI

What is it that wants only our rich dying,
When the light gets thin and seems to hold
Blue dusk, with sweet moon light all around
Sinking as the late light lives and dies?

When wings of closure flutter over us,
While drawing downward gravity grows jealous
To learn the tune of nature's quiet power,
As if impatient for history to take

Within itself the fading hue of a sky
From which all color is slowly dissolving
Into thin air? Before death's anthems
Are chanted, or time hangs its cloudy trophies

Down inside the warm breathing of things,
Till when like Orpheus I look back
As I leave you, elated yet uneasy in
The lightheadedness that sweeps over me,

No doubt appearing pale as my own ghost,
At the lone star fixed in splendor high above
The scene an unseen hand determines,
And gathering darkness swallows up the sky?

XII

High noon of brutal, relentless sun,
Cardinal hunting with a gun on the road,
Owl with a mirror fastened to its breast,
Lions aboard Bernini's broken boat,
Body parts of bandits impaled on poles,

Dusty carcasses of animals that hang
The black winds of the negative universe,
Trattoria where a crone in a black shawl
Appears to strum an unstrung lyre like
The letter seal given me by Fanny Brawne.

Swamp air and vapors wreathe the countryside,
Herdsmen poking at the skulls of horses,
Black the hue of mourning robes still drapes
Corporeal tissue decomposing
A week at market, darkening by degrees

From a faded terracotta red—the color
Steeps my brain in a dreamful fever-sleep,
Noon blasted by bolts of brass and gold
Wherein I labor beating out the links
Of fate, link after link, an endless chain.

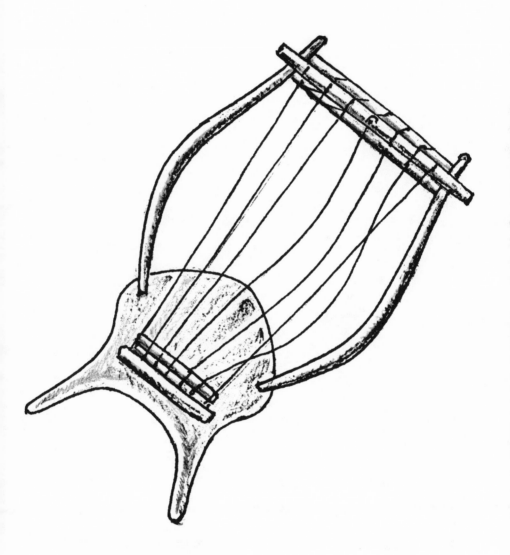

Printed January 1994 in Santa Barbara & Ann Arbor
for the Black Sparrow Press by Mackintosh
Typography & Edwards Brothers Inc. Text set in
Zapf by Words Worth. Design by Barbara Martin.
This edition is published in paper wrappers;
there are 200 hardcover trade copies;
100 hardcover copies have been numbered
& signed by the author; & 26 lettered copies
have been handbound in boards by Earle Gray,
each with an original drawing by Tom Clark.

Photo: Lina Todd

Tom Clark was born in Chicago in 1941 and educated at the Universities of Michigan (B.A.) and Cambridge (M.A.), publishing an undergraduate honors thesis on Ezra Pound in the *East–West Review*, 1963, and beginning that same year a ten year tenure as poetry editor of *The Paris Review*, introducing to the magazine such poets as Charles Olson, Robert Duncan, Allen Ginsberg, Frank O'Hara, John Ashbery and Ted Berrigan. His early verse collections *Stones* (1969) and *Air* (1970) were issued by Harper & Row; later selected poetry volumes appearing from Black Sparrow included *When Things Get Tough on Easy Street* (1978), *Paradise Resisted* (1984), *Disordered Ideas* (1987), *Fractured Karma* (1990) and *Sleepwalker's Fate* (1992). His *Junkets on a Sad Planet* is a poetic novel based on the life of John Keats; his other books on the lives of writers include *The Exile of Céline*, a novel, and biographical works on Damon Runyon, Jack Kerouac, Ted Berrigan, Charles Olson and Robert Creeley. His criticism on poetry has appeared regularly in the *San Francisco Chronicle* and other newspapers; the U. of Michigan issued a volume of those essays as *The Poetry Beat: Reviewing the Eighties.* Having spent the past twenty-five years residing in the American West—most of that time in California—he now makes his home in Berkeley.